Memes Nostalgia:

55 Hilarious Memes That Will Bring You Back In Time

Introduction

Do you have a lot of time to kill? Do you like to just sit back and have a mental pick me up at the end of your day? Or are you looking for great ideas of what to say no matter what situation arises?

No matter what it is that is motivating you, memes are the answer. They are funny, witty, and full of hilarious situations that we all face on a regular basis, but that we don't really know what to do this.

Tons of brilliant minds have put together a lot of different memes that are both sarcastic yet true. No matter what your situation is, and no matter what situation you are commenting on, no doubt there is a meme that has already been talking about it.

There are the common memes that we all know and love, then there are those that are new, but up and coming. Either way this is a great compilation of what you are looking for, and you will be sure to add this book to your favorites.

This book is your handy little compilation of all the memes that are popular today. 50 different hilarious memes that are sure to get you laughing all day long. Whether you are bored, looking for some entertainment, or are just looking for a funny thing to say, this is the book for you.

You will have a lot to say from what you see here, and even if you never use one in your real life, you will still have a lot to enjoy for yourself! So what are you waiting for? Let the entertainment begin.

The Best Meme's in 2015

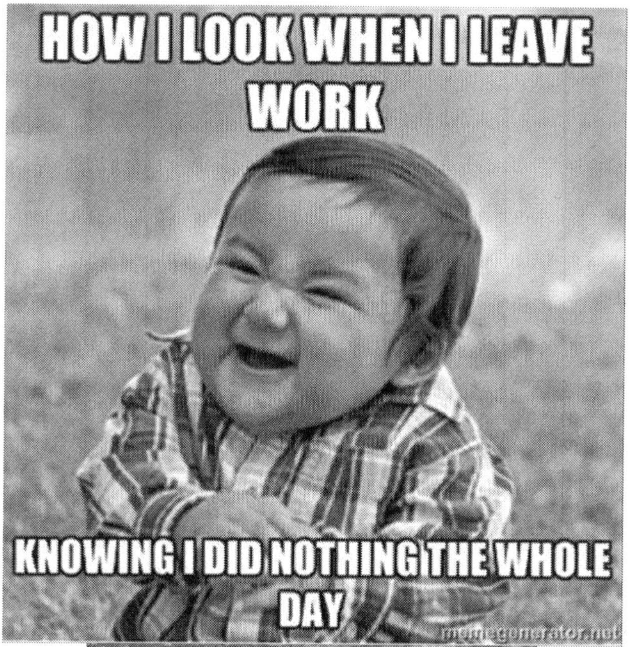
HOW I LOOK WHEN I LEAVE WORK
KNOWING I DID NOTHING THE WHOLE DAY

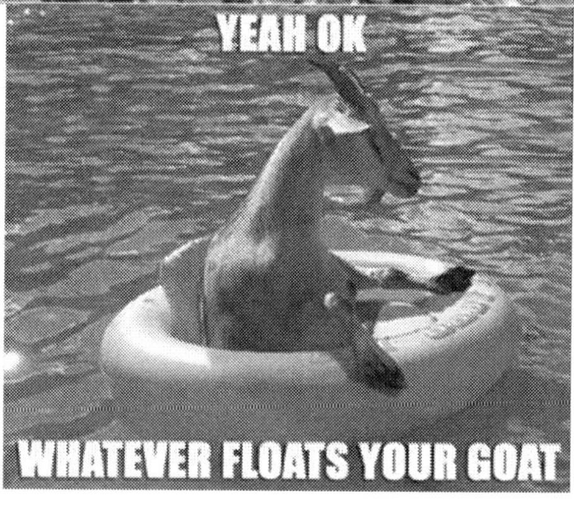
YEAH OK
WHATEVER FLOATS YOUR GOAT

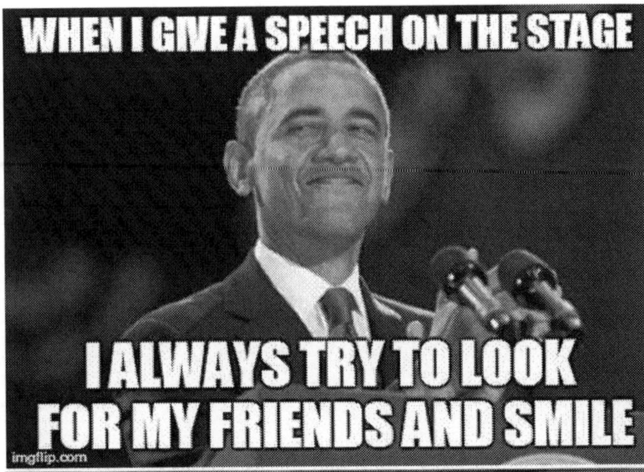
WHEN I GIVE A SPEECH ON THE STAGE
I ALWAYS TRY TO LOOK FOR MY FRIENDS AND SMILE
imgflip.com

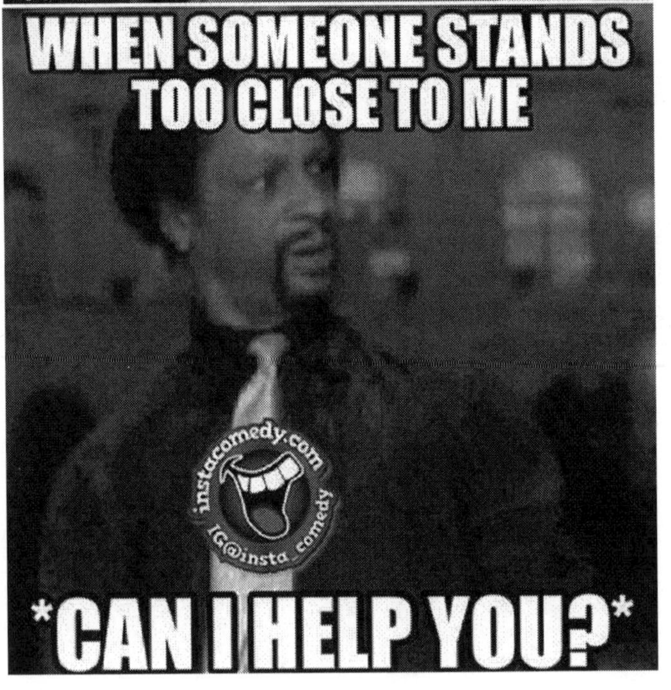
WHEN SOMEONE STANDS TOO CLOSE TO ME
instacomedy.com
IG@insta_comedy
CAN I HELP YOU?

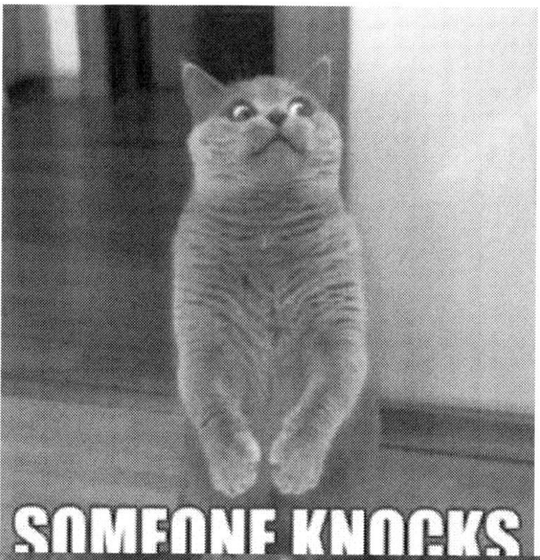
SOMEONE KNOCKS

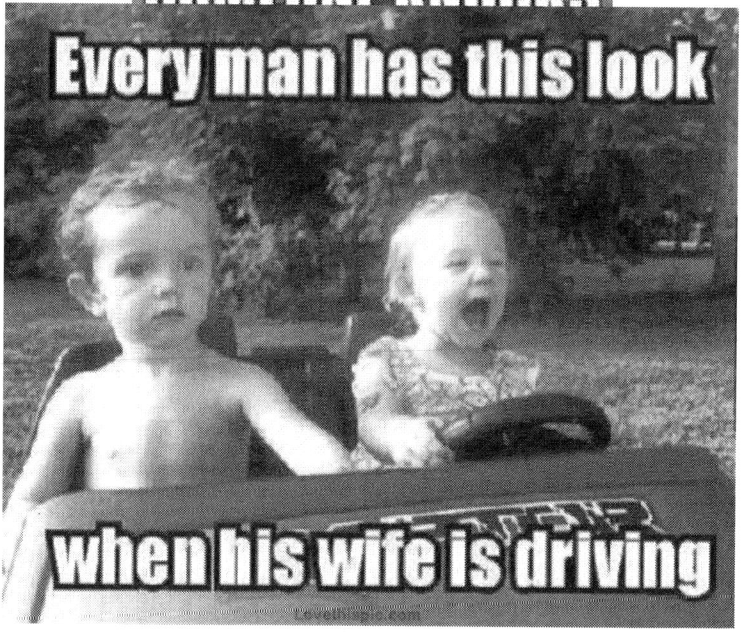
Every man has this look
when his wife is driving

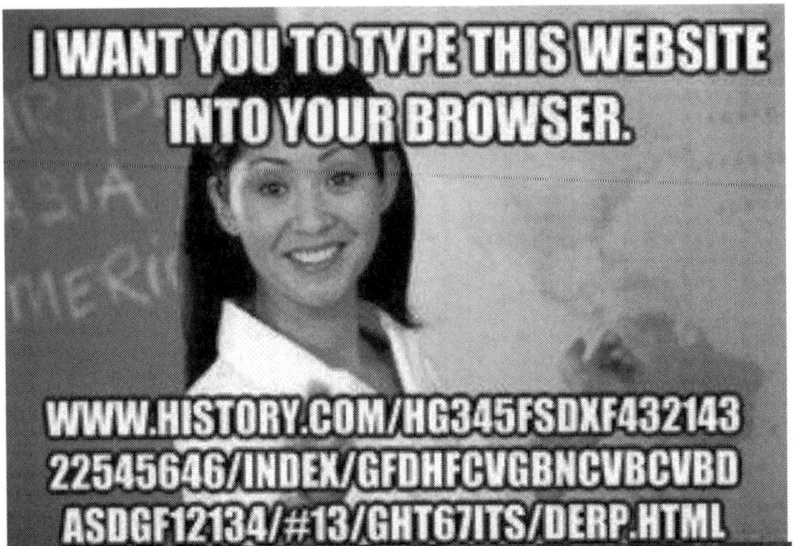

I WANT YOU TO TYPE THIS WEBSITE INTO YOUR BROWSER.

WWW.HISTORY.COM/HG345FSDXF432143 22545646/INDEX/GFDHFCVGBNCVBCVBD ASDGF12134/#13/GHT67ITS/DERP.HTML

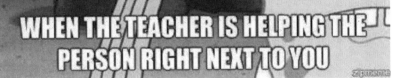

THAT AWKWARD MOMENT

WHEN THE TEACHER IS HELPING THE PERSON RIGHT NEXT TO YOU

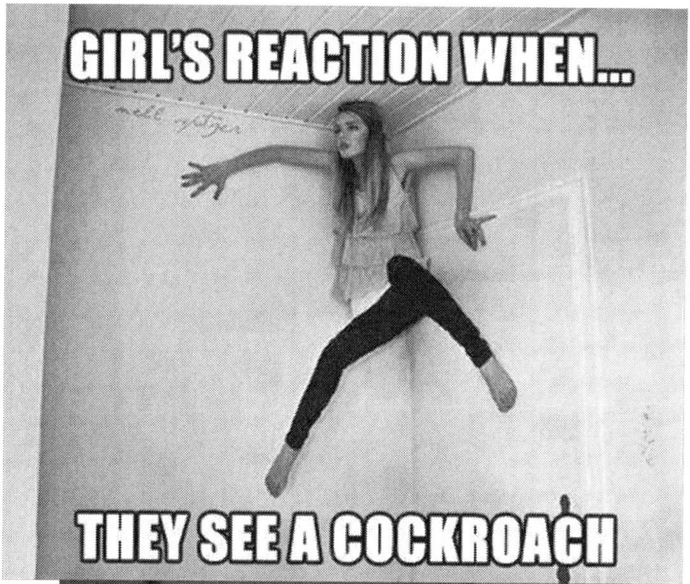
GIRL'S REACTION WHEN...
THEY SEE A COCKROACH
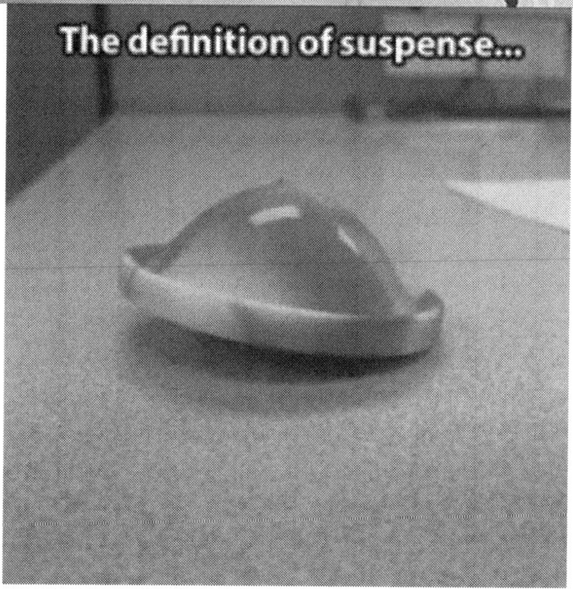
The definition of suspense...

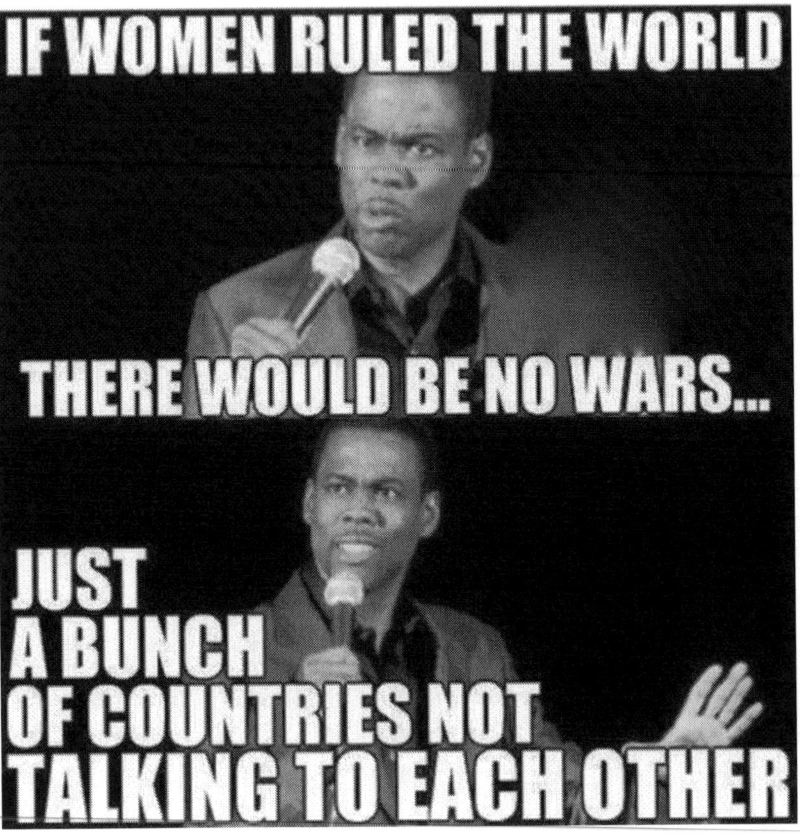
IF WOMEN RULED THE WORLD
THERE WOULD BE NO WARS...
JUST
A BUNCH
OF COUNTRIES NOT
TALKING TO EACH OTHER

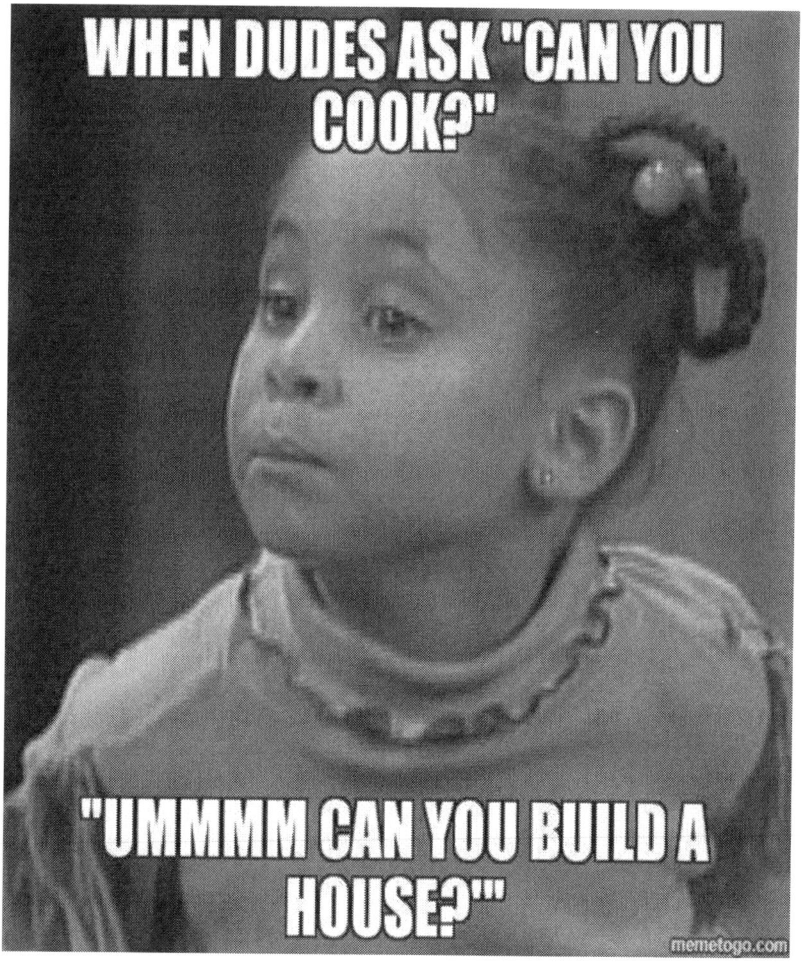
WHEN DUDES ASK "CAN YOU COOK?"
"UMMMM CAN YOU BUILD A HOUSE?"
memetogo.com

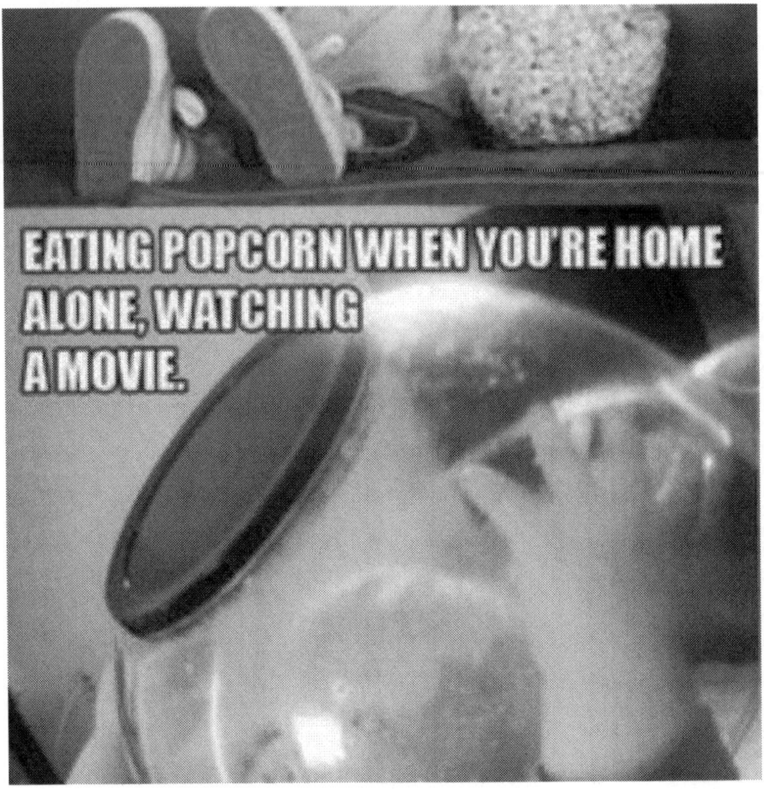
EATING POPCORN WHEN YOU'RE HOME
ALONE, WATCHING
A MOVIE.

WHEN CHURCH IS OVER AND
YOU TRYNA LEAVE
BUT YOUR MOM KEEPS TALKING

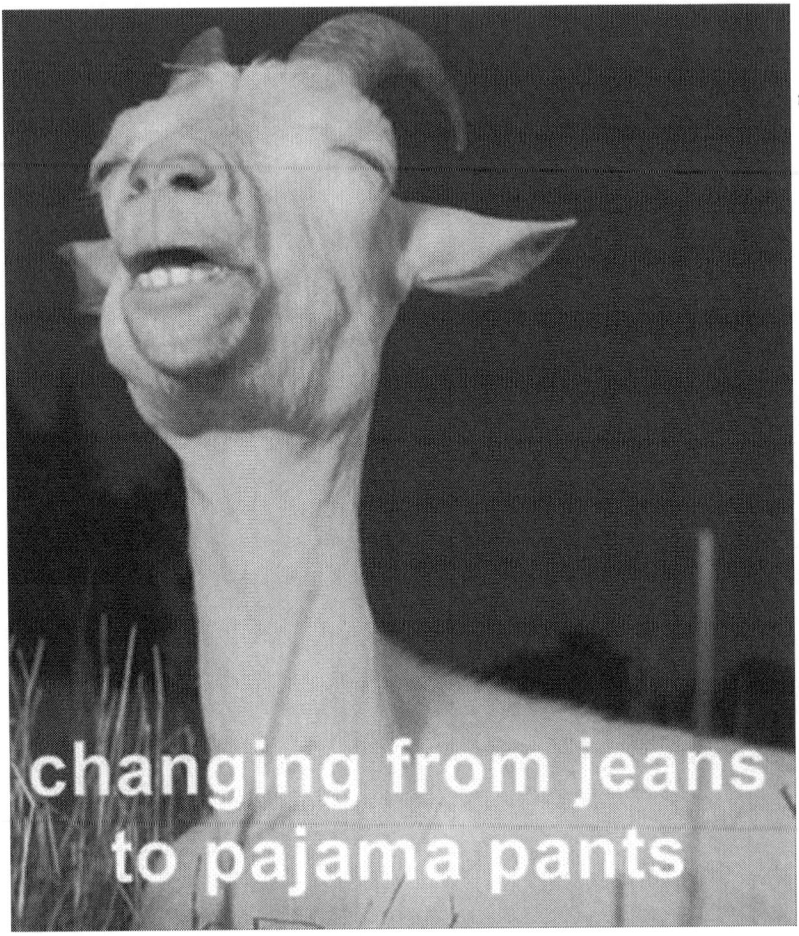
changing from jeans
to pajama pants

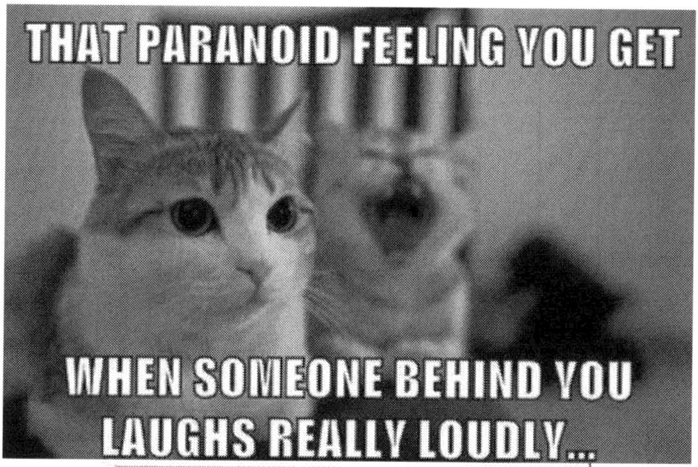
THAT PARANOID FEELING YOU GET
WHEN SOMEONE BEHIND YOU
LAUGHS REALLY LOUDLY...

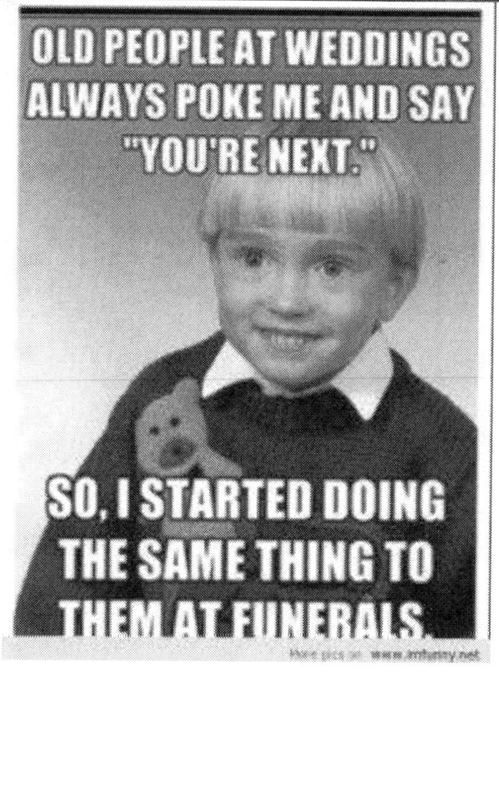
OLD PEOPLE AT WEDDINGS
ALWAYS POKE ME AND SAY
"YOU'RE NEXT."
SO, I STARTED DOING
THE SAME THING TO
THEM AT FUNERALS.

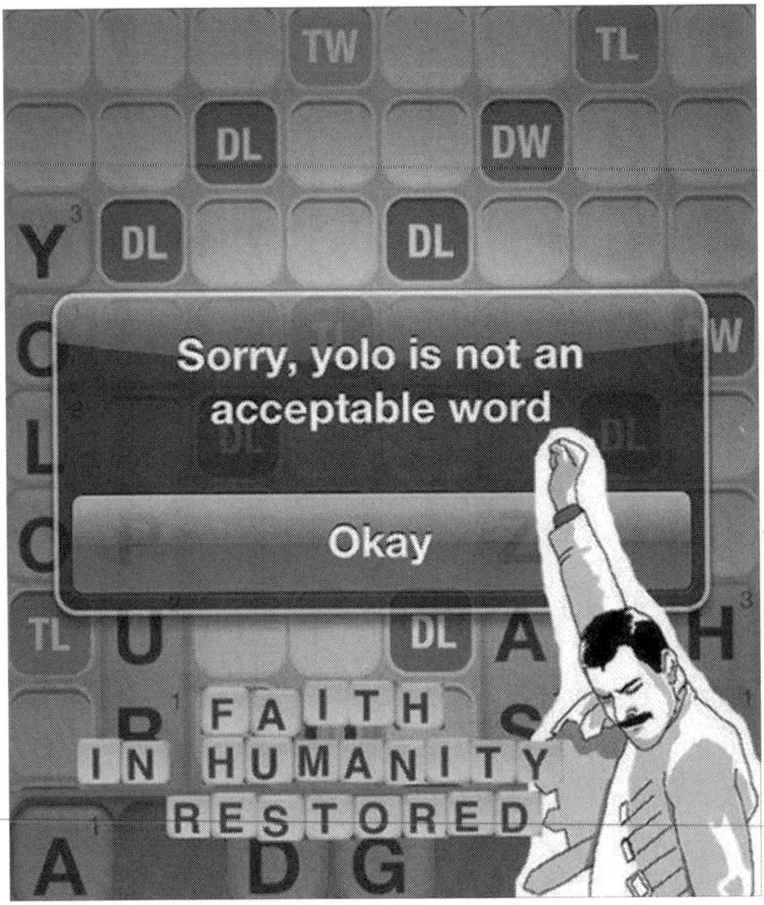
Sorry, yolo is not an acceptable word
Okay
FAITH
IN HUMANITY
RESTORED

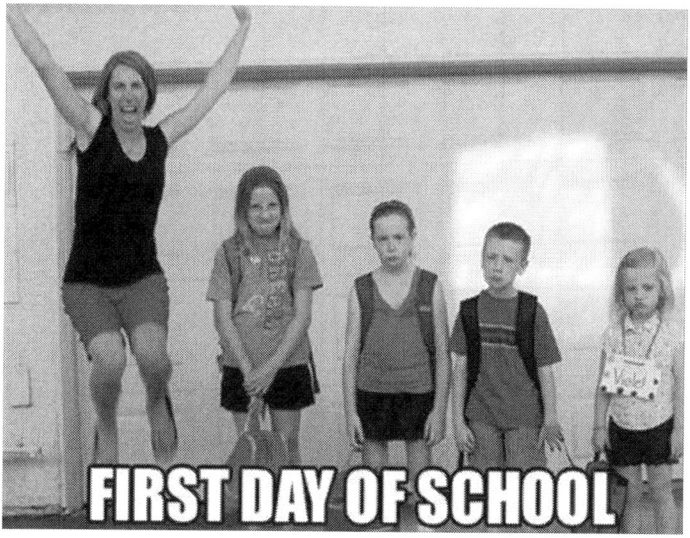
FIRST DAY OF SCHOOL

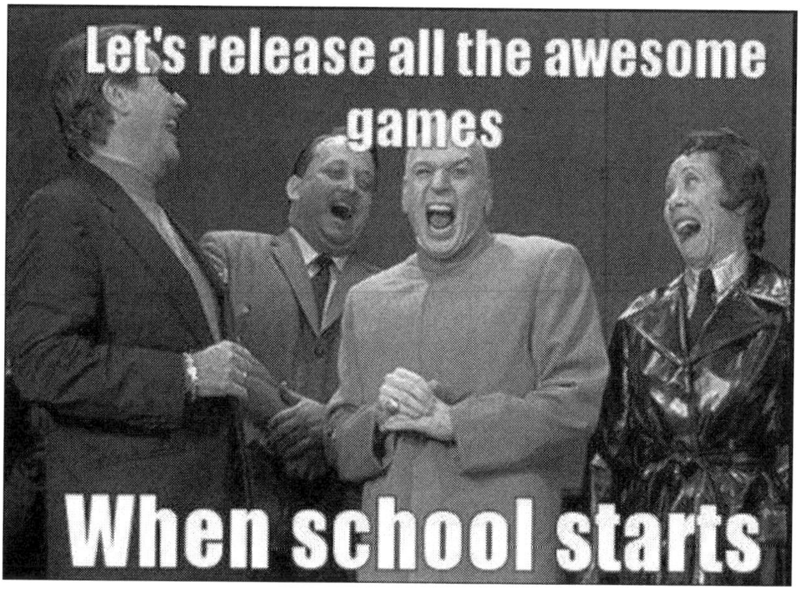
Let's release all the awesome games
When school starts

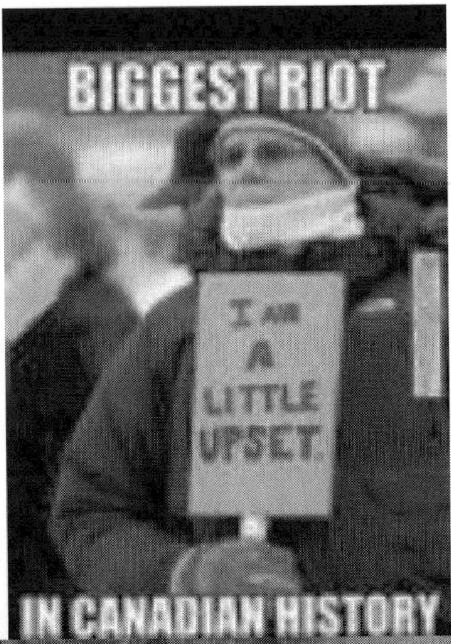
BIGGEST RIOT
I AM
A
LITTLE
UPSET.
IN CANADIAN HISTORY

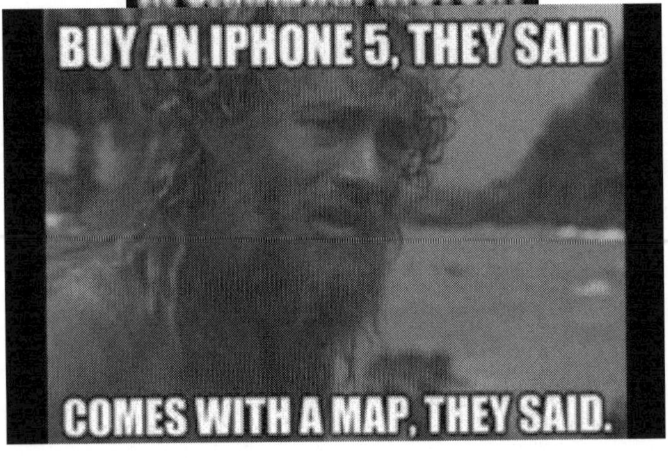
BUY AN IPHONE 5, THEY SAID
COMES WITH A MAP, THEY SAID.

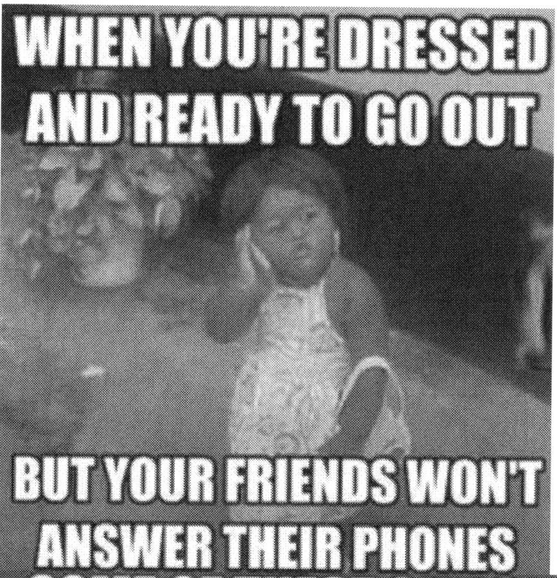
WHEN YOU'RE DRESSED
AND READY TO GO OUT
BUT YOUR FRIENDS WON'T
ANSWER THEIR PHONES

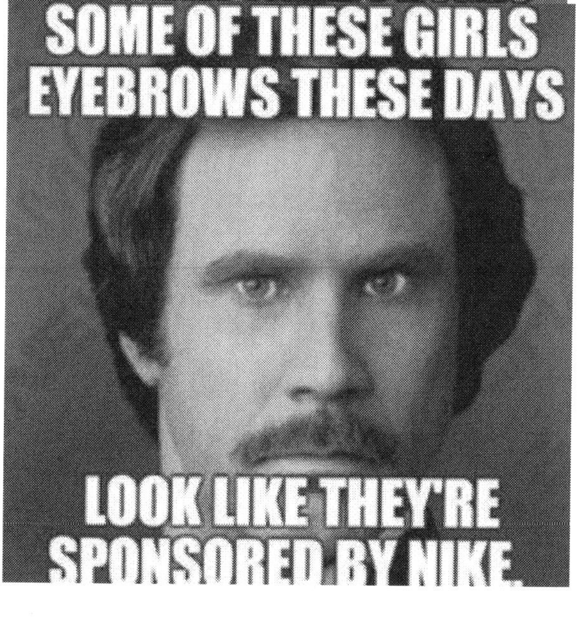
SOME OF THESE GIRLS
EYEBROWS THESE DAYS
LOOK LIKE THEY'RE
SPONSORED BY NIKE.

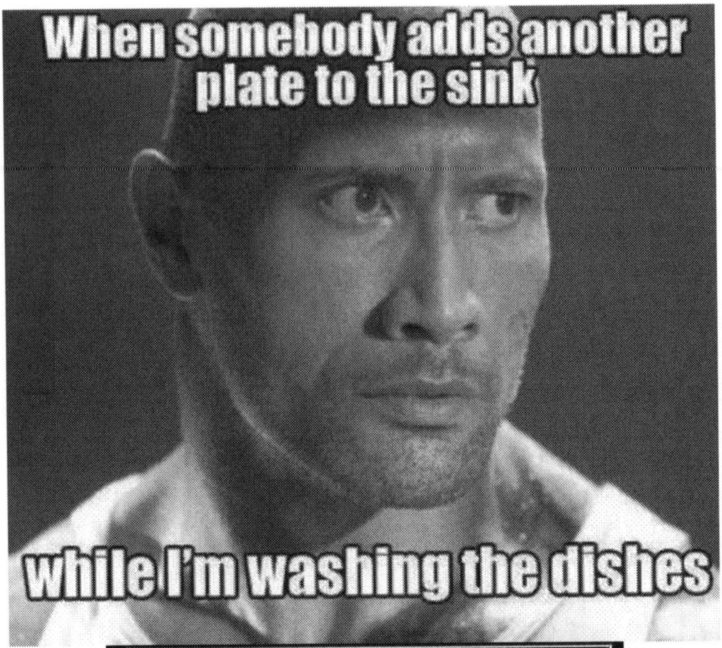
When somebody adds another plate to the sink
while I'm washing the dishes

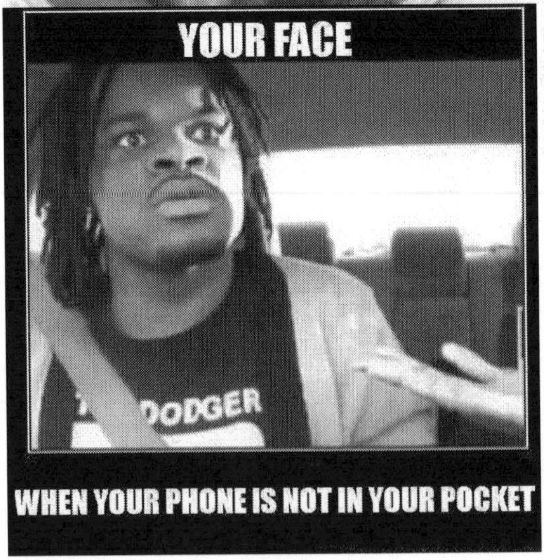
YOUR FACE
WHEN YOUR PHONE IS NOT IN YOUR POCKET

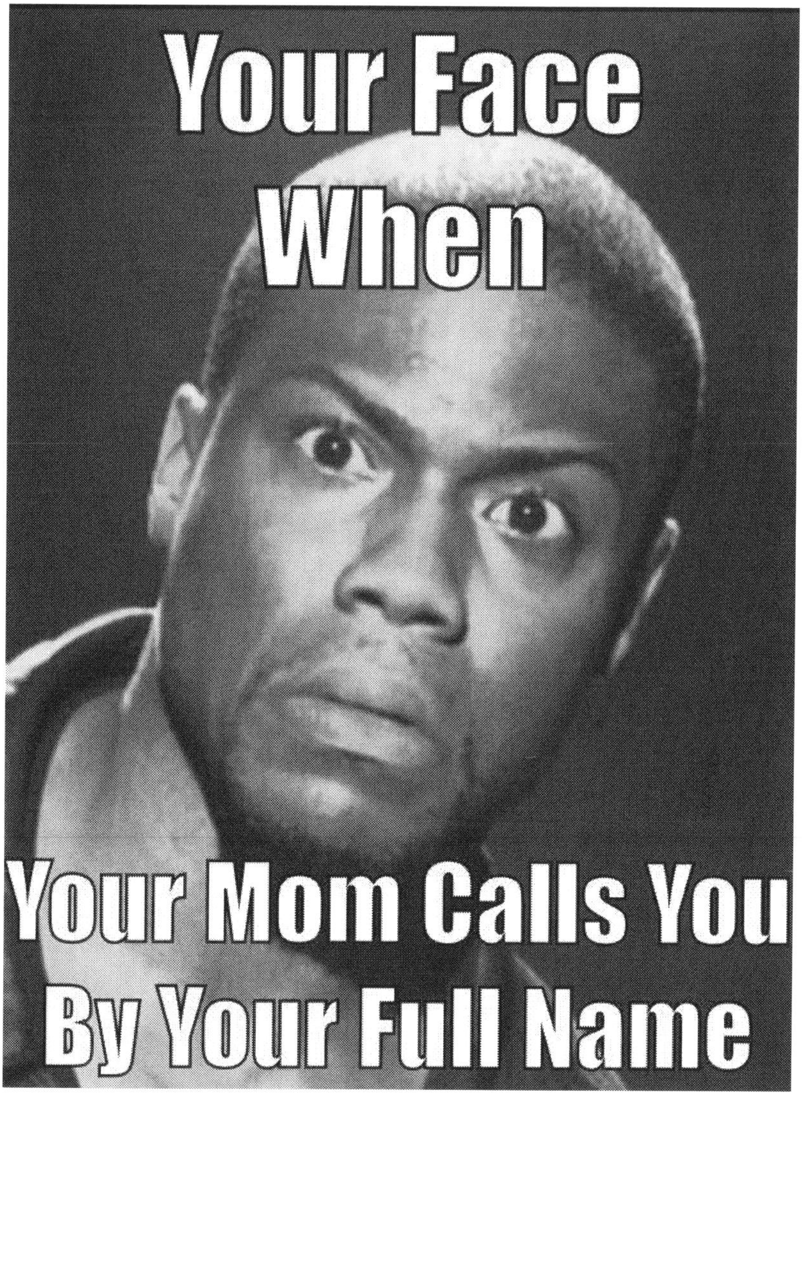
Your Face
When
Your Mom Calls You
By Your Full Name

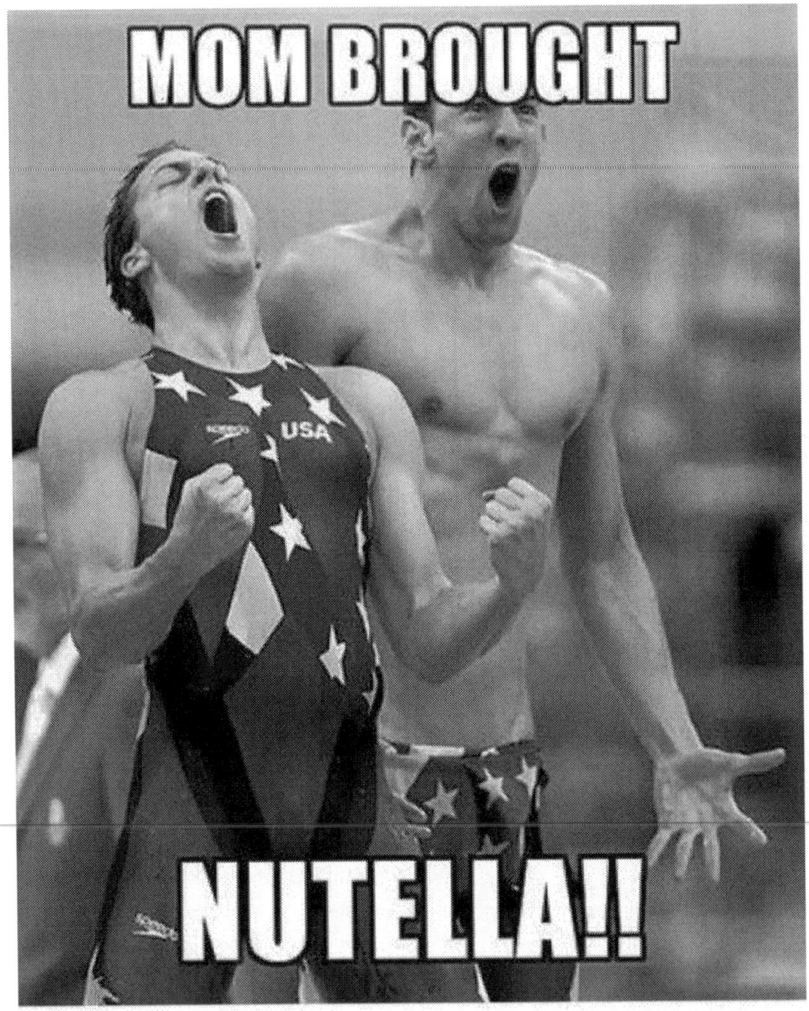
MOM BROUGHT
USA
NUTELLA!!

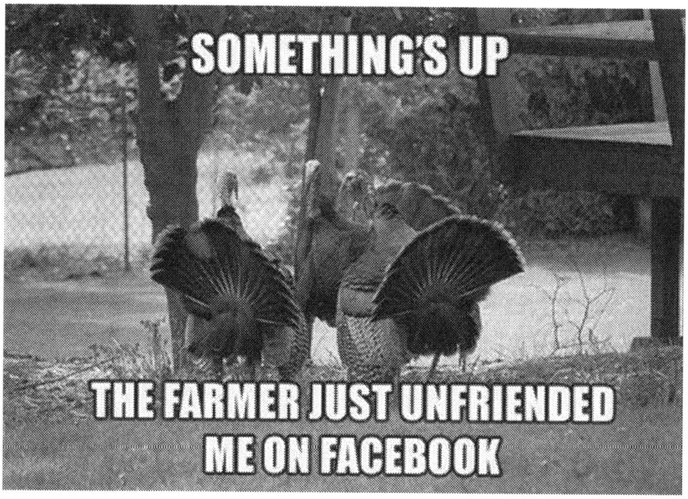
SOMETHING'S UP
THE FARMER JUST UNFRIENDED
ME ON FACEBOOK

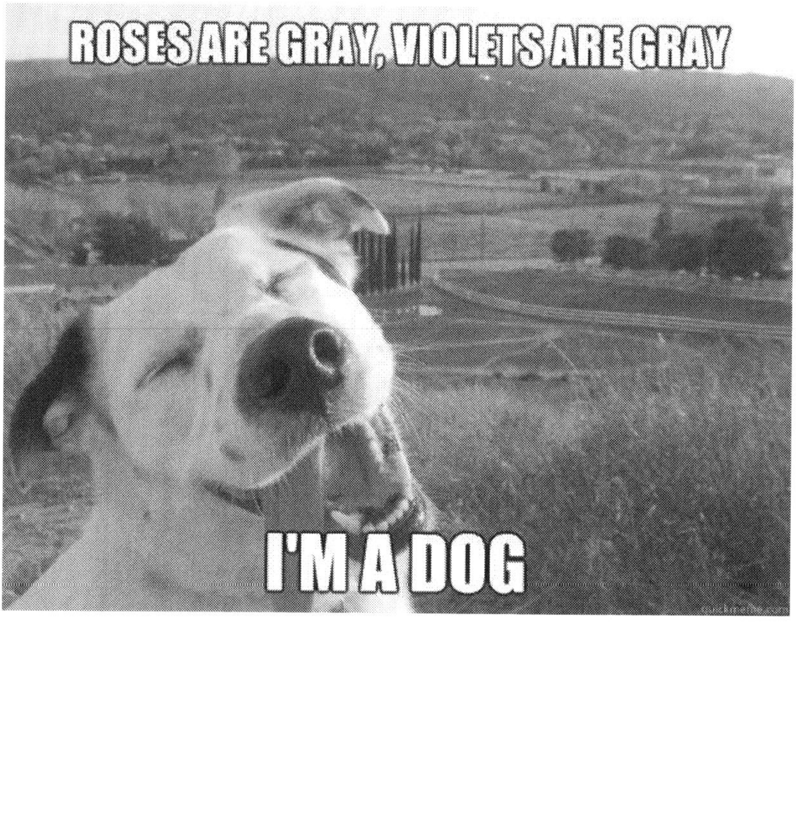
ROSES ARE GRAY, VIOLETS ARE GRAY
I'M A DOG

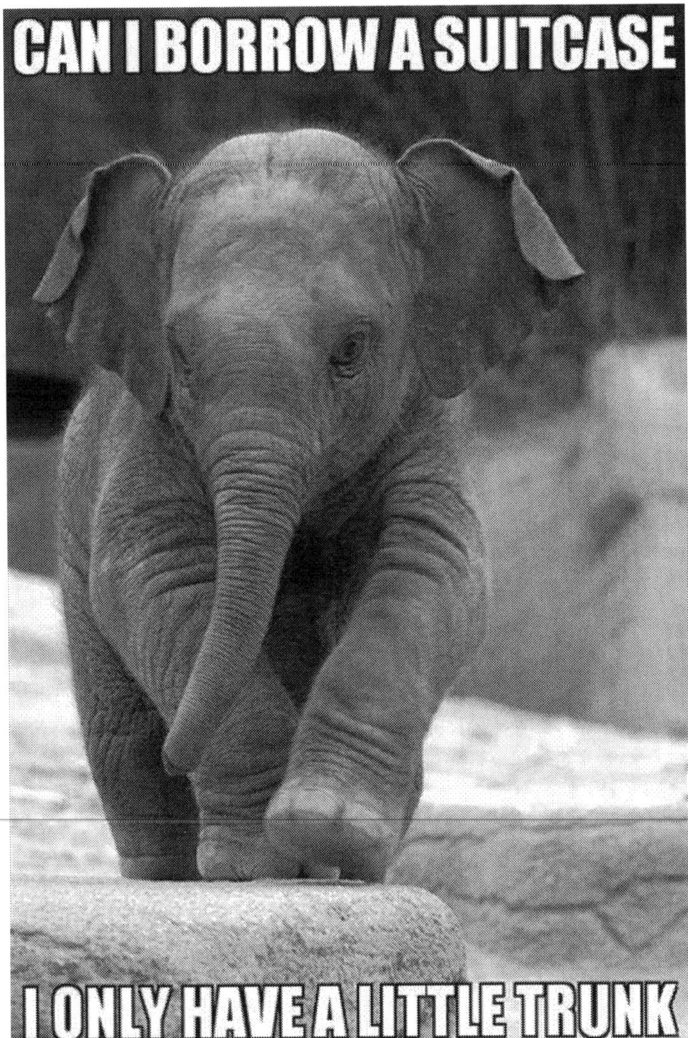
CAN I BORROW A SUITCASE
I ONLY HAVE A LITTLE TRUNK

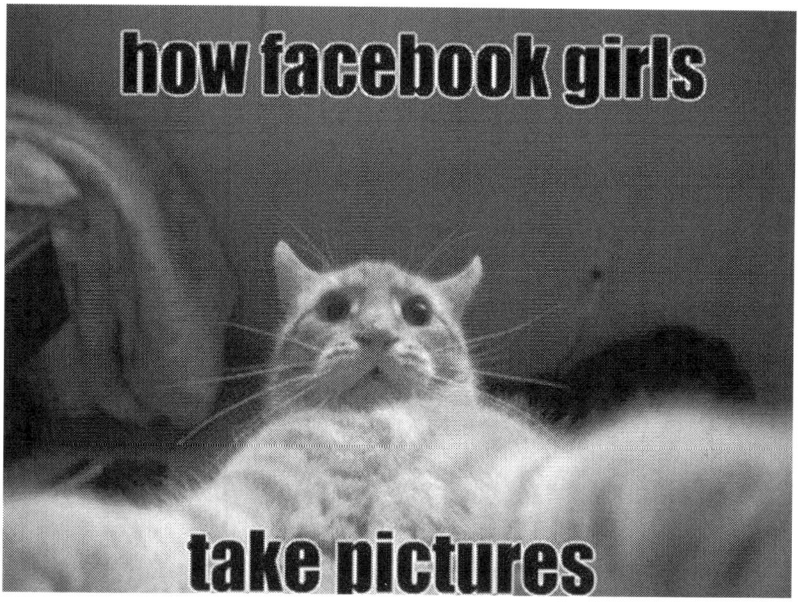
how facebook girls
take pictures

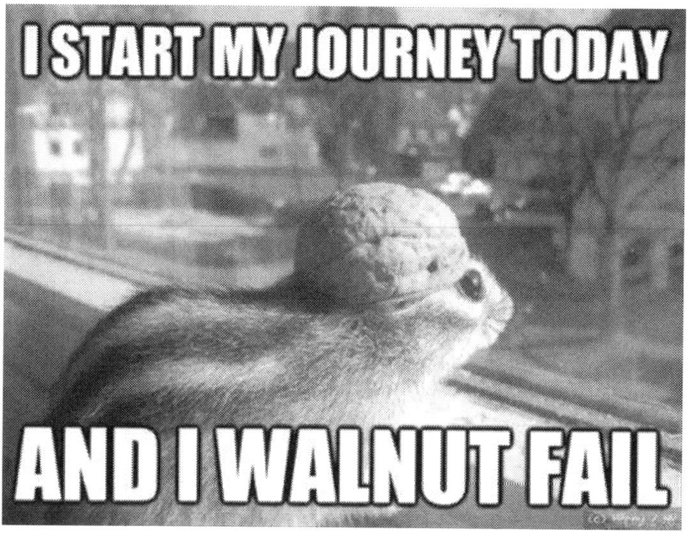
I START MY JOURNEY TODAY
AND I WALNUT FAIL

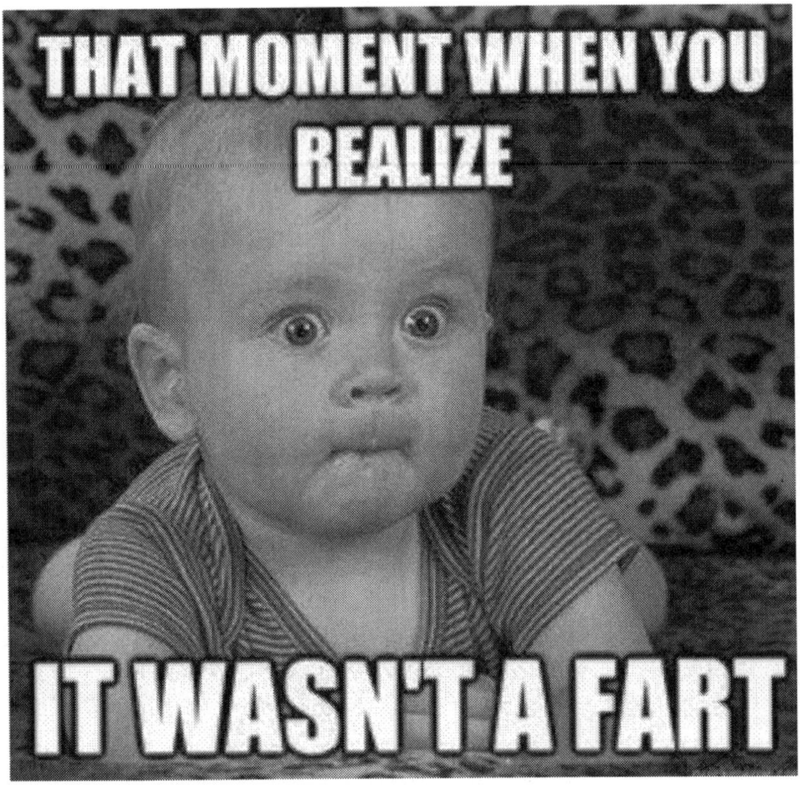
THAT MOMENT WHEN YOU
REALIZE
IT WASN'T A FART

ONE DOES NOT SIMPLY
KNOW HOW TO WORK A SHOWER AT A FRIEND'S HOUSE
memegenerator.net

I DON'T ALWAYS SAY SOMETHING STUPID
BUT WHEN I DO, I KEEP TALKING TO MAKE IT WORSE

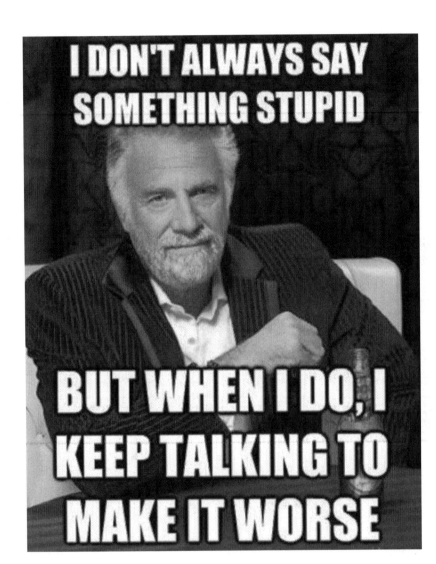

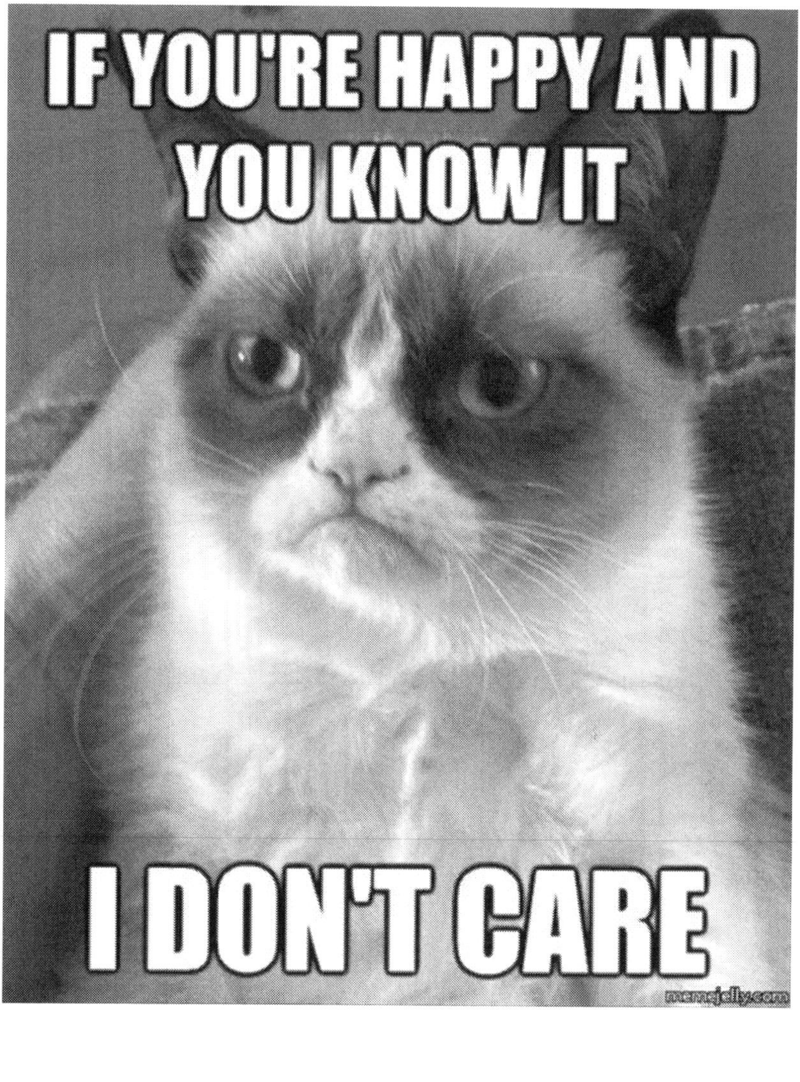
IF YOU'RE HAPPY AND
YOU KNOW IT
I DON'T CARE
memejelly.com

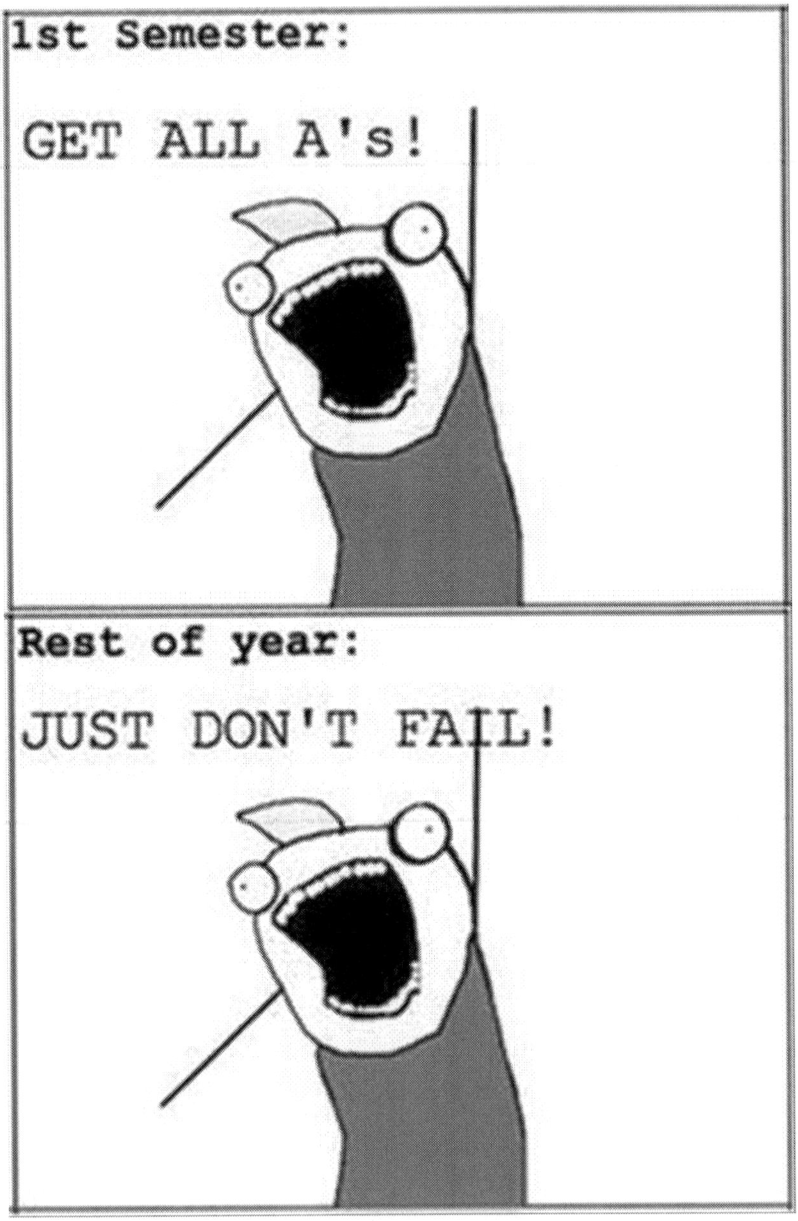
1st Semester:
GET ALL A's!
Rest of year:
JUST DON'T FAIL!

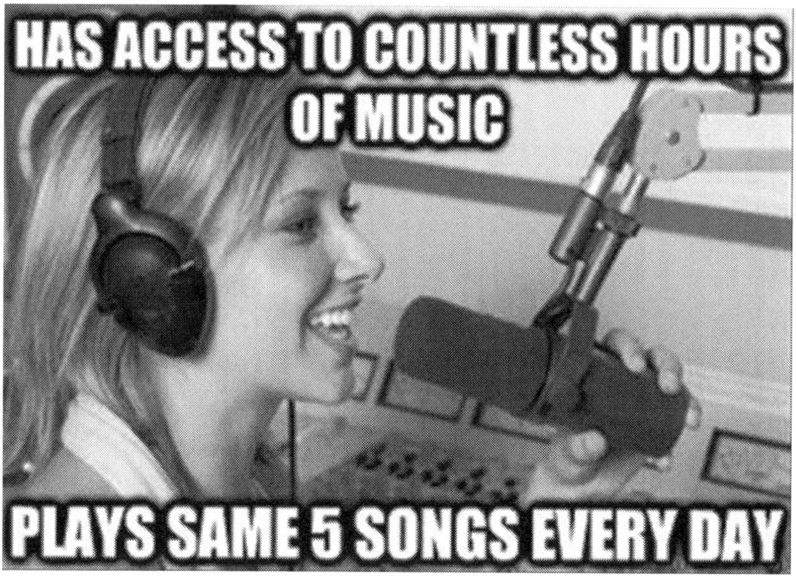
HAS ACCESS TO COUNTLESS HOURS OF MUSIC
PLAYS SAME 5 SONGS EVERY DAY

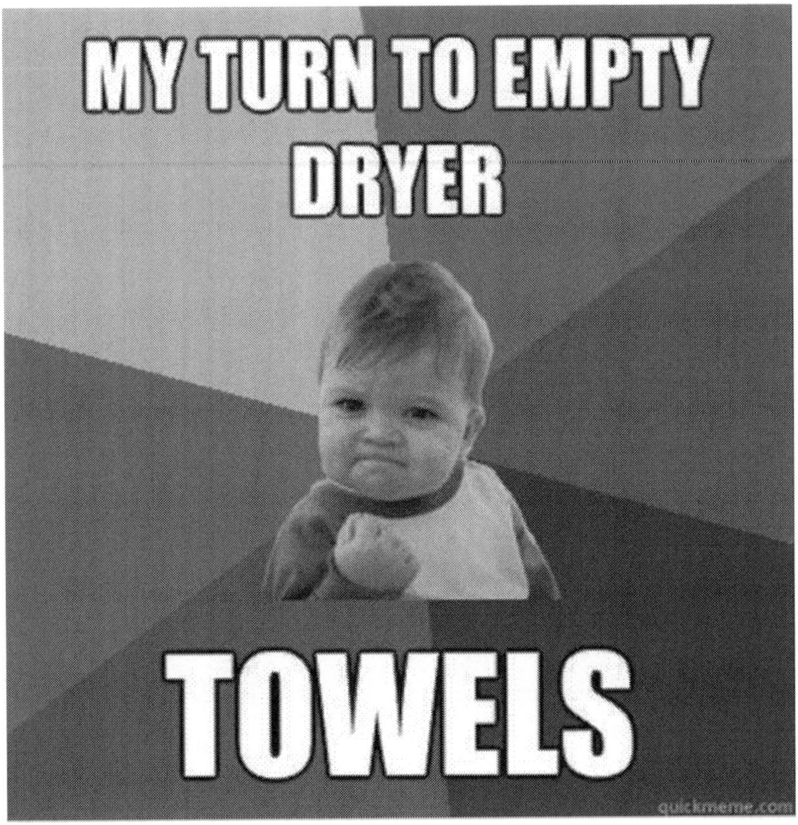
MY TURN TO EMPTY DRYER
TOWELS
quickmeme.com

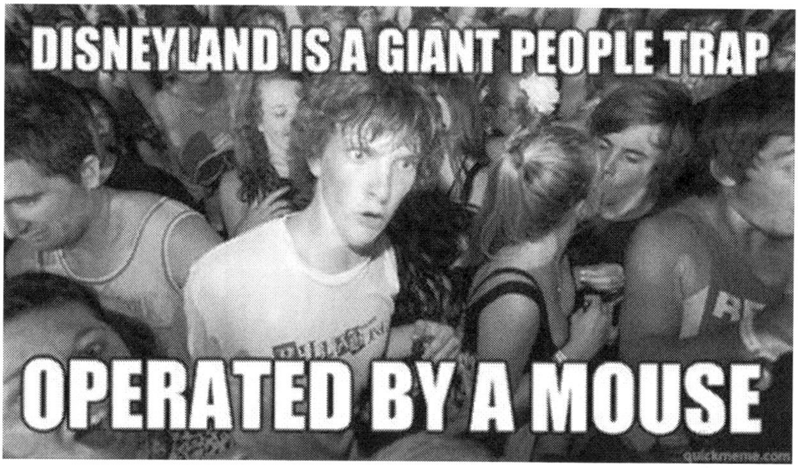
DISNEYLAND IS A GIANT PEOPLE TRAP
OPERATED BY A MOUSE
quickmeme.com

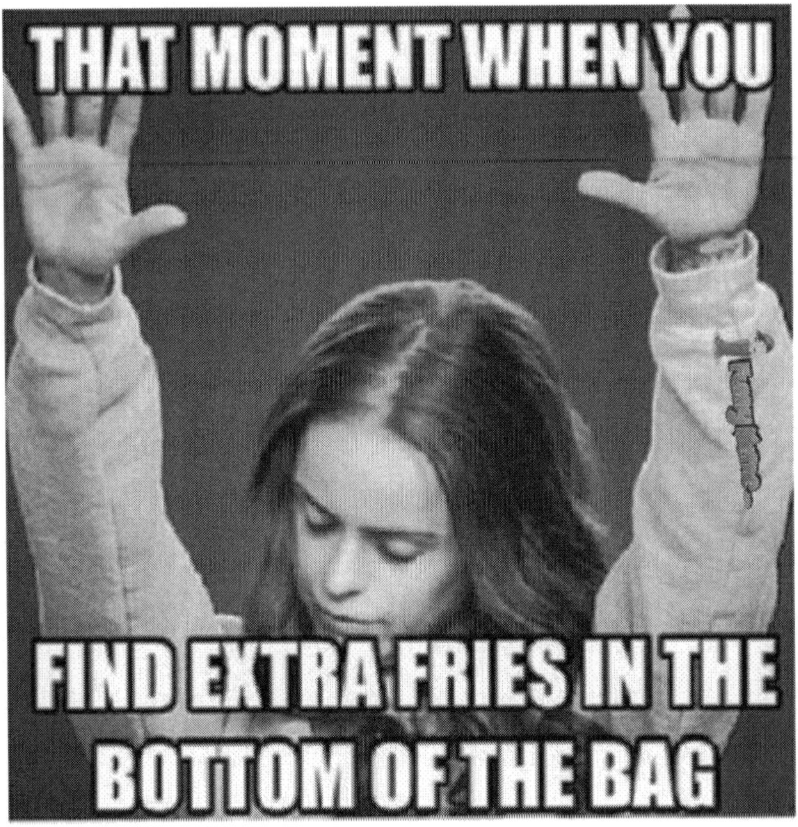
THAT MOMENT WHEN YOU
FIND EXTRA FRIES IN THE BOTTOM OF THE BAG

WHEN YOU

OPEN GUM AT
SCHOOL

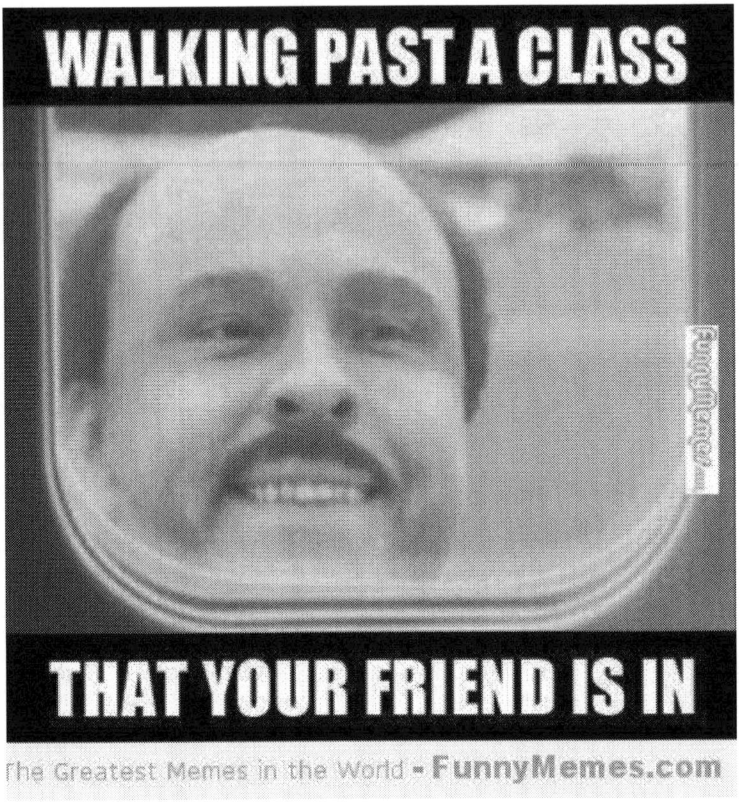
WALKING PAST A CLASS
THAT YOUR FRIEND IS IN
The Greatest Memes in the World - FunnyMemes.com

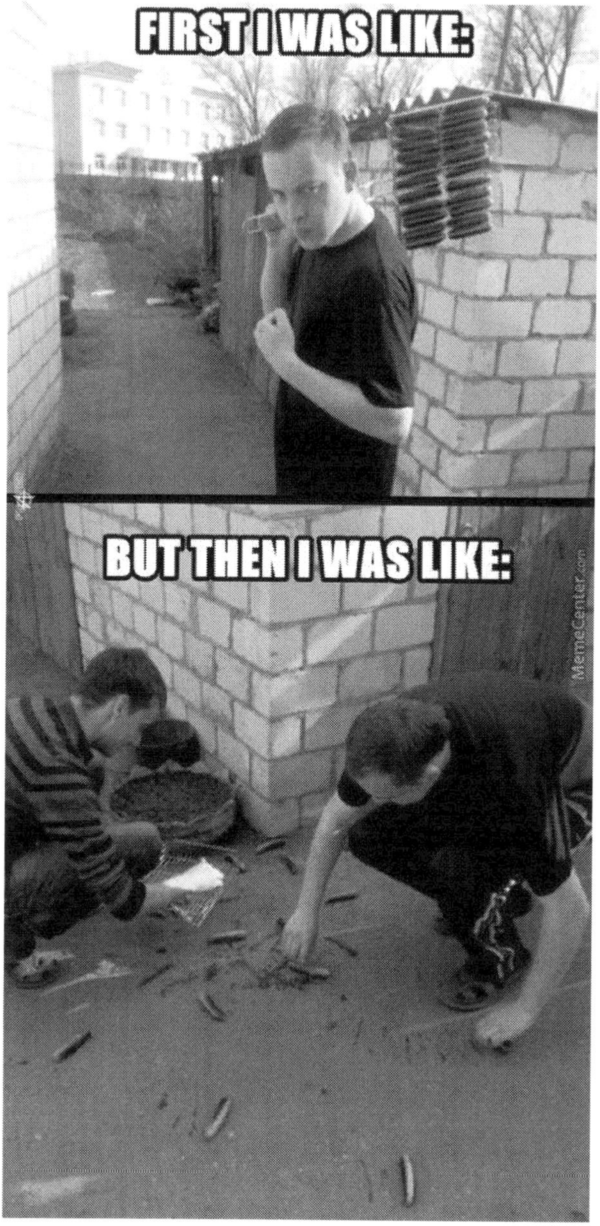
FIRST I WAS LIKE:
BUT THEN I WAS LIKE:
MemeCenter.com

Conclusion

There you have it, a wonderful compilation of some of the funniest of the current memes. All you need to do is grab yourself a cup of coffee, pull up your tablet, or other kindle device, and you are ready to settle in to a life full of laughter and good times.

Made in the USA
Monee, IL
26 September 2023

43424809R00022